Tea kettle of c.1750 with ornate tripod base and cane-covered swing handle. Similar designs are found in silver, but this one, made of cast brass and coated in silver, was a cheaper alternative.

BRASS AND BRASSWARE

David J. Eveleigh

Shire Publications Ltd

CONTENTS

Published in 1995 by Shire Publications Ltd,
Cromwell House, Church Street, Princes Ris-
borough, Buckinghamshire HP27 9AA, UK.
Copyright © 1995 by David J. Eveleigh. First
edition 1995. Shire Album 311. ISBN 0 7478
0274 2.
David J. Eveleigh is hereby identified as the
author of this work in accordance with Section
77 of the Copyright, Designs and Patents Act
1988.

Printed in Great Britain by CIT Printing Services, Press Buildings, Merlins Bridge, Haverford-
west, Dyfed SA61 1XF.

British Library Cataloguing in Publication Data. Eveleigh, David J. Brass and Brassware. –
(Shire Albums; No. 311). I. Title. II. Series. 739.520941. ISBN 0-7478-0274-2.

ACKNOWLEDGEMENTS
Illustrations are acknowledged as follows: Bristol City Museum and Art Gallery, pages 9
(top), 20; Roderick Butler, pages 6 (top), 9 (bottom); the Rural History Centre, University of
Reading, pages 10 (bottom), 16, 19 (bottom), 25 (right), 26 (bottom left); Sotheby's, Sussex,
pages 1, 11 (bottom); the Victoria and Albert Museum, pages 3, 5. All others are acknow-
ledged to Blaise Castle House Museum. The zinc content of the brass in the photographs on
pages 4 (bottom), 8 and 13 (top) is taken from analyses performed by D. Hooke and P. T.
Craddock of the Department of Scientific Research, the British Museum. I am also grateful to
Paul Craddock and Joan Day for their comments and also to Stephen Price for help with the
Birmingham industry.

Cover: *Lid from a late seventeenth-century warming pan. The tulip design, similar to those
found on delftware chargers of c.1680-1700, has been created by piercing and engraving the
sheet brass. (Photograph by Andy Cotton.)*

*Brass plaque marking the office of churchwarden held by Thomas Paddon in the parish of Zeal
Monachorum, Devon, dated 1705 and made by Lewes Pridham, a clockmaker in nearby
Sandford in the first half of the eighteenth century.*

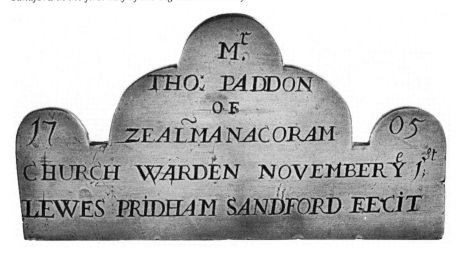

Brass 'detector' lock by John Wilkes of Birmingham (died 1733). A catch swings the man's leg forward to reveal the keyhole and point his toe to an odd number on the inner ring. When the key is turned, the dial rotates so that the number of times the door was opened could be checked.

THE ORIGINS OF ENGLISH BRASS

Brass is a metal of many uses and many associations: 'brassy', 'not worth a brass farthing' and brass bands are just three terms associated with the metal. They attest to the versatility of brass and also to its popularity, especially as an inexpensive substitute for gold, which it superficially resembles.

Brass also has a long history: it was known to the Romans and by the twelfth century its manufacture was well established on the continent. By the sixteenth century brass wire was required to make wool cards, used to straighten the fleece before spinning. Brass ordnance was employed in the nation's defence and, in the field of science, astrolabes, used in navigation and astronomy, were made of brass. Brass was also widely used in the home, particularly in the kitchen, as hundreds of

household inventories confirm. Thus the 1633 inventory of Thomas Dorny, a yeoman farmer of Stoke Gifford, north of Bristol, records two brass pots, four brass kettles, one small brass pan, one skillet, one brass ladle, two brass candlesticks and a spice mortar, valued at £2 16s 0d, in the kitchen.

However, the word 'brass' was then used generally to describe any yellow-coloured alloy of copper, including those containing lead and tin, and it was only in the mid eighteenth century, at least in the western world, that brass came to be recognised as an alloy of copper and zinc. Zinc was little known or understood in Europe before the sixteenth century: it could not be obtained by conventional smelting from the ore as the metal boils at 917°C, which is below the temperature required to smelt the ore. Instead, brass was made by heating calamine, an ore of zinc, with broken copper. This process, known as *cementation*, was recorded as early as *c.*1130 by Theophilus, a German monk, but the alloying of the two metals was not understood and neither was calamine recognised as an ore of zinc: it was simply believed that calamine gave copper weight and colour.

The chief centres of the medieval industry were in Germany and the Low Countries, close to reserves of calamine and on river sites where water power was used to hammer the sheet brass into finished goods – pans and dishes – called *batteryware*, and also to make brass wire. The working of the brass demanded considerable skill and the works substantial capital investment. There is little evidence for brass production in England before the sixteenth century. All the brass used for church memorials from the thirteenth century was supplied from the continent. Copper-alloy goods were made by English craftsmen in medieval towns using imported raw materials and sheet brass called *latten*, although until the early

Small brass lock, probably from a case or trunk, dated 1640.

eighteenth century their output was probably insignificant compared to the large quantities of brassware shipped from the

Chestnut roaster, sheet brass riveted to a wrought-iron handle. The lid exhibits superb pierced and repoussé ornament, which is almost certainly Dutch. The gadrooning around the rim suggests a date of c.1690. Analysis has shown the brass contains 30.47 per cent of zinc, achieved either by using granulated copper in the calamine process or by adding zinc metal.

4

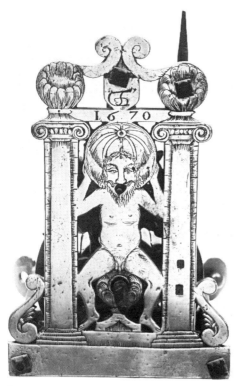

Face plate of a weight-driven roasting jack for turning the spit, showing Hercules supporting the globe. Cast brass, dated 1670.

made, at Isleworth on the Thames in Middlesex; this met with greater success and here brass which would 'abide by the hammer' to make kettles and pans was first made in England.

This and subsequent attempts to establish English brassmaking during the seventeenth century were clearly stifled by the lack of native skill and the system of Crown monopolies, and imports of finished brass goods remained high. Then in 1689, with the English copper and brass industry struggling to survive, the Crown relinquished its monopoly on mining and brass production with the passing of the Mines Royal Act.

Almost immediately there was renewed interest in the mining and smelting of copper. By 1694 copper ore from Cornwall was being smelted at Conham, 2 miles (3 km) east of Bristol on the river Avon. In *c.*1702 Abraham Darby started brass production at Baptist Mills on the river Frome in Bristol. Soon additional mills at Keynsham and Saltford on the Avon were making batteryware and brass wire.

Although free of the restrictions of royal monopolies, the Bristol brass company did encounter some of the difficulties which had dogged earlier ventures and held back the expansion of the English brass industry. One problem was the shortage of skilled labour, which had to be solved by hiring workers from the Low Countries. More tellingly perhaps, early Bristol brass was held to be 'hard, flawy and scurfy' and thus difficult to work. Continental brass was preferred; moreover, the trade with the continent was well established and the imported brass enjoyed low duties.

Facing stiff competition, the Bristol makers in 1712 petitioned Parliament to raise the duties on imported brass: this provoked braziers in London, Norwich and elsewhere to counter-petition, testifying to the superiority of foreign brass over English.

After a comprehensive enquiry the

Low Countries. Inventories occasionally refer to Flemish ware: for example, the 1663 Lichfield inventory of Margaret Fenton lists a 'Flanders kettle' along with other brass utensils in the buttery.

In the 1560s substantial deposits of copper ore were discovered near Keswick in Cumbria and calamine was found on the Mendips in Somerset. In 1568 the Mines Royal Company was granted a royal monopoly to mine and smelt copper and, in the same year, the sole right to mine calamine and manufacture brass was granted to the Mineral and Battery Works. Both companies relied heavily on continental investment and expertise, the Mineral and Battery Works on a Saxon zinc miner, Christopher Schutz, who, with the aid of workers from Germany, established brass works at Tintern on the river Wye in Gwent. Unfortunately, the brass was not malleable enough to be worked into battery and production was soon abandoned. In 1582 a second attempt was

Tobacco box of sheet brass with engraved decoration and dated 1720.

government decided not to raise the duties on imported brass, but despite this the Bristol industry ultimately prospered where others had failed. Several major advantages favoured the development of the brass industry in the Bristol area. Above all, the city occupied an unrivalled location: there was ample water power and the bulky raw materials were close at hand. The calamine was brought from the nearby Mendips and a regular supply of copper was shipped from Cornwall. The use, for the first time, of the reverberatory furnace was also crucial to success in Bristol: it enabled the copper to be smelted using coal, which was available from local collieries at half the price it fetched elsewhere, and ultimately led to a better-quality metal. The Bristol company soon built its own copper works at Crew's Hole and the copper produced there went to the brass-smelting works at Baptist Mills.

In spite of foreign competition, the Bristol company found a ready local market for its products. Significantly, the workers of brass in Bristol had not joined the

Dog collar, sheet brass, inscribed 'Chisorton Read, Butcher, Shambles, Bristol, 1751'.

Measure for a 'Wine Quart of a Pinte', dated 1677, showing the arms and monogram of Charles II (top) and the arms of the City of Bristol (bottom). Cast in a pale yellow copper alloy, probably containing tin or lead.

protest against the home-produced metal and had emphasised their satisfaction with the quality of the locally made brass, claiming that it was at least 20 shillings per hundredweight cheaper than the metal they formerly obtained from Holland. Other markets included the pin makers in Gloucester and the burgeoning industry in Birmingham. Brassware could also easily be exported through the port of

Bristol: so-called 'Guinea kettles' were taken by slave traders on the outward leg of their voyage for barter in West Africa.

From the start the Bristol industry was financed by wealthy Quaker businessmen. One of them, Nehemiah Champion, in 1723 patented a new method of making brass using granulated instead of broken copper. The old cementation process would not produce a brass containing more than 28 per cent zinc but in a granulated form the copper was able to absorb the zinc more readily. Champion claimed that his modified process would increase the zinc content from 28.6 per cent to 33.3 per cent. Thus for a given weight of copper more brass was produced and, copper being by far the most expensive constituent, Champion's innovation also undoubtedly contributed to the success of the Bristol industry.

Champion's patent of 1723 also marked an important step in the growing appreciation of the crucial relationship of zinc to brass and in 1738 William Champion, a son of Nehemiah, patented a method of producing zinc from calamine by distillation. Champion's patent followed several years of investigations on the continent, where metallic zinc had been imported in small quantities from the Far East since the mid sixteenth century.

Nevertheless, William Champion was the first to make zinc, or 'spelter' as it became known, on a large scale in Europe. The relationship between zinc and brass was now fully understood but the impact of Champion's innovation on brass was at first limited. The obstacle was financial: metallic zinc was expensive, considerably more so than calamine; it was not commercially viable to use metallic zinc except in small quantities to produce high-copper alloys – the so-called 'gilding metals', such as pinchbeck and tombac, which were used in Birmingham for the production of 'toys' (buttons, buckles and items of jewellery). Much of Champion's zinc went straight to Birmingham: it was simply uneconomical to produce the great bulk of brass with metallic zinc.

These technical developments were accompanied by the continued expansion of the industry. In 1746 William Champion had established a second company in the Bristol area, 2 miles (3 km) east of the city at Warmley, where extensive works produced copper, brass and zinc. Elsewhere, the Cheadle Copper and Brass Company started brass production at Cheadle in Staffordshire in 1719 and another major venture, Roe and Company, started production in Macclesfield, Cheshire, in 1757. All three centres produced brass in sheet and ingot form along with wire and batteryware. Wire went to the pin makers in Gloucester, Cheadle sent ingot brass to Sheffield and all supplied Birmingham. By 1740 the importation of continental brass had virtually ceased. Britain was now self-sufficient in brass and rapidly seizing the technological and commercial initiative from the rest of Europe.

Battery pan raised from sheet by water-powered hammers. The rim is stamped 'Bristol Battery Co'. The zinc content is 37.34 per cent, probably dating the pan to after the 1830s, when the Bristol company replaced cementation with brass made by direct mixing of copper and zinc. Batteryware was made by the company until 1908.

Skillet cast in pot-metal by Clemant Tosear, a Salisbury bell and pot founder active from c.1679 to 1717.

FOUNDERS, BRAZIERS AND COPPERSMITHS

At their peak during the eighteenth century, the brassmaking companies in Bristol and elsewhere manufactured a small range of finished goods but much of their output was left as sheet or ingot brass or wire. This was supplied to braziers, founders and other specialist tradesmen, such as button and buckle makers, who used the brass to make a vast range of finished brassware for domestic and industrial use.

The two industries were thus closely related but nevertheless were distinguished by differences in organisation: whilst brassmaking operated on a large scale with considerable investment of capital, the production of brassware was mostly in the hands of small independent tradesmen. They typically worked in cramped workshops attached to their homes and employed no more than a few apprentices and journeymen (hired craftsmen). Another difference was that brassmaking was concentrated at a few locations, usually close to the supply of raw materials, whilst braziers and founders were widely distributed throughout Britain.

Founders made objects by casting (pouring molten copper alloys into moulds), whilst the brazier wrought goods by hand from sheet metal. Founders and braziers were recognised as separate trades and in large towns were organised into their own guilds or companies which controlled and regulated business. In London, companies for both trades were established in the fourteenth century. In

Cauldron cast in pot-metal, dated 1675.

9

Spoon, cast brass and originally tinned, with seal-top handle characteristic of the late sixteenth century. The maker's mark of two inverted spoons is stamped on the bowl.

practice the distinctions were less clear. Founders and braziers commonly worked together, the brazier being responsible for the finishing and assembly of cast brassware.

Founders cast in several different alloys of copper. From the twelfth century bells were cast from bronze, an alloy of copper and tin. Domestic utensils, such as cauldrons, skillets and mortars, were made from an alloy often erroneously called 'bell-metal' which was actually a high lead-copper alloy with only a small quantity of tin. To contemporaries, this dull, pale yellow metal was known as 'crock brass' or 'pot-metal' – the metal of cooking crocks. A similar alloy, also called pot-metal, with a lead content as high as 20 per cent, remained in use in the mid nineteenth century for the casting of cocks (taps). Bell and pot founding shared similar casting techniques; the moulds were made of clay mixed with dung and fre-

The casting house, from Charles Tomlinson's 'Cyclopedia of Useful Arts and Manufactures', 1853. The man in the background is lifting a crucible of molten brass with iron tongs from the furnace while the man in the foreground pours the contents into a mould at an angle. The men are wearing handkerchiefs over their faces to keep out the dense fumes of zinc oxide released during casting.

Mortar and pestle, cast brass.

cooking pots, and they were sometimes known as potters.

A continuous development of casting in brass proper – the alloy of copper and zinc – can be traced to *c*.1680 in Bristol and to the 1690s in Birmingham and elsewhere in the West Midlands. However, its origins in England probably date to the previous century. From *c*.1560 in London spoons were being cast in brass containing about 25 per cent zinc. By the mid seventeenth century candlesticks with a flared circular base, the 'trumpet-based' type, were being cast in England. Nevertheless the large-scale expansion of brassfounding dates from the late seventeenth century. By using moulds of sand in place of clay, cheaper castings were possible and from this time the range of cast brass goods increased dramatically.

Brass used in casting was called yellow

Tankards of cast brass originally silvered. The baluster-shaped bodies, scroll thumbpiece and domed lid are typical of the period c.1760.

quently the two trades were combined. Edmund Giles of Lewes in East Sussex, John and Thomas Palmar of Canterbury and Clemant Tosear of Salisbury were four of several well-known seventeenth-century bellfounders who also made skillets cast with their names. Other founders, such as John Fathers of Montacute in Somerset, confined their production to

brass as inventories from the late seventeenth century confirm. The 1733 inventory of a Bristol founder, William Neast, provides a detailed picture of brassfoundry equipment and materials of the period. Neast had started business only several years earlier but his workshop contained over ninety different finished articles. Most were everyday things: tea

Right: *Contrasting candlesticks of c.1750. (Left) A plain example with a push-up device to remove the candle stump. (Right) An ornate design similar to styles in silver. Both were made by casting the stem in two hollow sections which were then brazed together, a technique in use between c.1700 and c.1780. The vertical seam on both is just discernible to the naked eye.*

Left: *String box of cast brass, late eighteenth century.*

Below: *Candle-snuffers, cast brass, eighteenth century.*

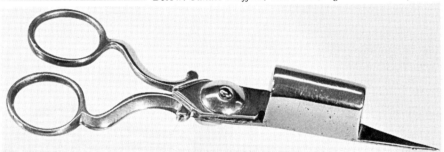

kettles, candlesticks and furnishing accessories such as door knockers, curtain rings and handles of various kinds. His working materials included pewter, copper, pot-metal, yellow brass, wire and 'shruff' – scrap metal and file dust from the workshop floor which was remelted. The inventory includes details of his tools and equipment: a moulding trough, bellows and patterns made of lead and brass.

Patterns were the masters from which copies were cast. They were invaluable, therefore, to the founder and their quality governed the quality of the castings. Moulds were made by packing sand around the pattern in a rectangular frame of wood or iron. The frames were made in two halves which could be separated in order to remove the pattern. A channel called a *runner* was cut through the sand to enable the molten metal to reach the impression. Finer channels called *risers* were also made so that hot air and gases could escape when the hot metal entered the mould. Hollow objects such as pots and taps required core moulds to create the interior and these had to be positioned in the mould with great care. The brass was heated in a crucible made of some fire-resistant material such as fireclay; Neast owned eighteen such 'melting pots'. At a temperature of 1000°C the brass

12

Roasting jacks with cast brass face plates and brass gears. (Left) A jack of c.1790, almost entirely made of brass. (Right) A jack of c.1775 made by Richard Eva, a clockmaker of Tregony, Cornwall; the brass has a zinc content of 23.86 per cent.

melted and was then poured into the mould.

When the metal had cooled, the mould was broken away by the *fettler*; the runners and risers, resulting from brass cooling in the channels, were broken off and then, using a lathe or file, all roughness was smoothed off. Neast's workshop housed two lathes, five vices and 'about 3 dozen files'. Finishing brassware was noisy, uncomfortable work. In his *Survey of London*, first published in 1598, John Stowe writes of the 'loathsome noise' caused by the 'turning and scrating' of brass articles being finished by the founders of Lothbury. It was also unhealthy: copper and brass dust in the workshops turned the hair of workers green and was also the cause of serious chest diseases.

Braziers shared these risks to health. As they worked with sheet metal, their tools were similar to those used by a general smith. Edward Cockey, a Bristol brazier who died in 1637, left a vice, a pair of shears and a soldering iron along with 'other small tools'. Similar equipment was found in the workshop of Thomas Westell, another Bristol brazier, in 1727. He also had twenty-eight hammers, a swage block used to create special shapes in the metal, a parcel of sets and punches, old files, rasps, marking irons and forge bellows.

The techniques of the brazier were relatively simple. The metal was cut out

Goffering-iron stand of cast brass.

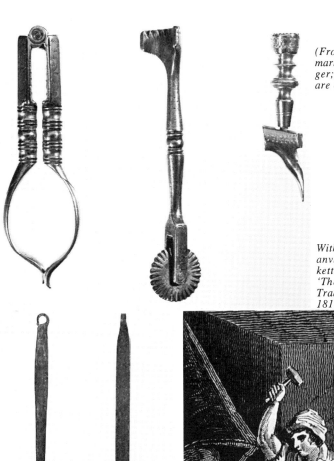

(From left) Nut crackers marked 'T. B.'; pastry jigger; tobacco stopper. All are cast brass.

With forge, hammer and anvil the brazier raises kettles and pans. From 'The Book of English Trades', seventh edition, 1818.

Ladles of sheet brass riveted to handles of wrought iron.

Simple spout oil lamp of sheet brass with a weighted base and jointed lid.

Below: *Candle box, sheet brass.*

with shears and hammered into shape; then the various parts were soldered or riveted together. Braziers often decorated their work by piercing and fretwork; punches were used to stamp stars, circles and create wrigglework – patterns of broken or zigzag lines. Designs in relief were achieved by mounting one layer of brass over another, or by raising decoration from the reverse using punches – a technique known as *repoussé* work, much favoured by silversmiths. Unlike the sophisticated work of the silversmith, however, the vigorous art of the brazier was firmly rooted in the traditions of English folk or vernacular art. The subjects which embellish seventeenth-century warming-pan lids – tulips, animals, human figures and armorial devices – are also found on slipware and delftware pottery of the period. Inscriptions, such as 'In God is all My Strength', are also found on warming pans, and owner's inscriptions generally are not uncommon on sheet-brass articles. Maker's marks, however, are rare and so the craftsmen responsible for much of this hand-wrought brassware, notable for its individuality, remain largely unknown.

Curfew of sheet brass with pierced, overlaid and repoussé ornament, used to cover the embers on the hearth at night. Seventeenth century.

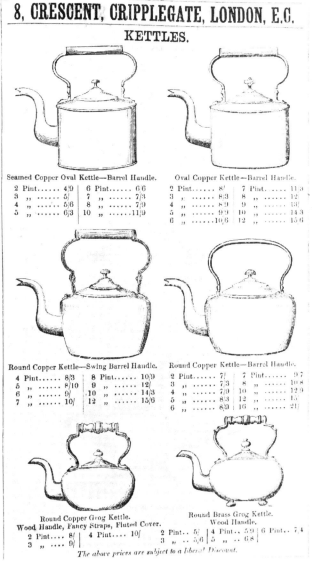

Kettles in copper and brass advertised by Warner of the Cripplegate Foundry, London, in 'The Ironmonger', 28th February 1861.

Braziers commonly undertook repairs and often worked in association with coppersmiths, tinsmiths and pewterers. The techniques of coppersmithing were very similar. Working in sheet metal, coppersmiths made kitchen utensils of copper but were concerned chiefly with the production of industrial equipment such as boilers and vats for brewing, cheese-making and sugar refining.

From the late eighteenth century the quality and individual character of sheet brassware declined as the role of the brazier as a producer of finished goods was overtaken by the advent of machine stamping. By the nineteenth century, the brazier was often no more than a retailer of brass and other metal goods.

Stock pot of sheet copper with cast brass tap made by A. G. Williams & Company, brassfounders and coppersmiths in Bristol from 1868 to 1892.

The brazier mending kettles and warming pans. From 'Little Jack of All Trades', 1810.

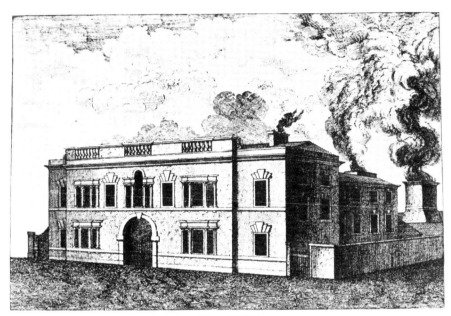

Turner's Brass House, Birmingham, established 1740.

THE RISE OF THE BIRMINGHAM INDUSTRY

The improved supplies of English brass after 1700 stimulated the expansion of the trades producing finished brassware in London, Bristol and elsewhere. Nowhere, however, was the expansion as dramatic as in Birmingham.

By the seventeenth century Birmingham was already established as a centre for skilled metalwork. Locksmiths and buckle and button makers in the town were using brass before the end of the seventeenth century and brassfounding was established there in the 1690s. After 1700 the numbers of brassfounders, in particular, increased rapidly but they remained dependent on brass made elsewhere; poor communications and the shortage of water power hindered the development of brassmaking in the town. In the early eighteenth century foreign supplies gave way to brass from the Bristol and Cheadle companies. Then, in 1740, Turner's Brass House was established in Coleshill Street – the first brassmaking works in Birmingham.

The brass companies in Bristol and Cheadle attempted to ruin Turner's enterprise by undercutting his prices. Although they failed, Turner was forced to join a combination formed by the existing companies and later joined by Charles Roe of Macclesfield. The combination imposed its prices on the market, leaving the Birmingham makers at their mercy. In 1780, responding to an increase in the price of Cornish ore, the combination raised the price of brass from £72 to £84 per ton. There was outrage amongst the brassworkers in Birmingham. Their response was swift and decisive. In 1780, by a cooperative effort, they established a new company, the Birmingham Metal Company, and, encouraged by the recent improvements in communications to the city, decided to build brassworks beside the canal in Broad Street. Using steam power and cheap copper ore from the huge reserves recently discovered at Parys Mountain in Anglesey, the Birmingham workers finally asserted their independence from

Patterns for brass drop handles from a brass stamper's pattern book of c.1800.

the combination. Although they continued to supply the Birmingham market, the old companies entered a slow decline.

The new Birmingham works continued to make brass by the cementation method, although in 1781 James Emerson, a Bristol maker, patented a new method of producing brass using metallic zinc in place of calamine. This produced brass which was said to be 'more malleable, more beautiful and of a colour more resembling gold than ordinary brass'. Unfortunately it was expensive and by 1803 Emerson was bankrupt. In the first half of the nineteenth century, however, the price of zinc fell by roughly a half as more foreign zinc entered Britain and the brassfounders turned to making their own brass by direct mixing of copper and zinc.

As the physical properties of brass vary according to the proportion of zinc in the metal, the direct method of brassmaking enabled foundries to adjust the alloy to suit different needs. This was the key to the versatility of the metal. Brasses with small quantities of zinc – up to about 15 per cent – are reddish in colour and were widely

Candlestick of cast brass made by John Moffat, brassfounder, chamber and pillar candlestick and snuffer maker of Scotlands Works, Birmingham from c.1849 to 1860.

The manufacture of brass clockwork roasting jacks was mainly centred on Birmingham. This is Restell's patent jack, introduced by E. B. Bennett & Sons (successors to John Linwood) of St Paul's Square, Birmingham, c.1850.

used in jewellery. Ordinary yellow brass, containing about 30 per cent zinc, is a strong malleable metal which also casts easily. With more zinc the metal becomes harder and less malleable, and more than 40 per cent zinc produces a hard brittle alloy, whiter in colour.

By the end of the eighteenth century there were about fifty brass manufacturers in Birmingham. Some were general founders producing a wide range of domestic fittings, bell-hanging equipment and cabinet brassfoundry – accessories for cabinet makers and carpenters. There was, nevertheless, a considerable degree of specialisation which was not found elsewhere. The different types of brasses used and the expertise involved in pattern and mould making encouraged specialisation in a particular product. Cock founders, for example, of whom there were six by 1780, made various types of taps and favoured the use of pot-metal containing copper, zinc and lead because it was easier to turn on the lathe. Moreover, preparation of the complicated patterns and core moulds used in cock founding required considerable skill.

Brass candlestick making was another distinct branch of the Birmingham industry which had emerged by the 1770s. Until improvements in oil and gas lighting in the nineteenth century, candles remained the commonest source of artificial light and candlesticks were made in a variety of materials ranging from wood and iron to silver. Brass candlesticks bridged the gap between the two: some designs followed closely the fashions set by silversmiths; others were plain and functional. Chamber sticks, wall sconces and lanterns were usually made of sheet brass.

Other specialist Birmingham metalworkers such as locksmiths, scale makers and roasting-jack makers made use of brass. Roasting jacks were mechanical devices for turning the spit in front of the fire and had many working parts of brass. Weight-driven jacks, which were common in the eighteenth century, often had decorative face plates of cast brass, sometimes engraved with the maker's name and a date. Clockwork bottle jacks, so called from the shape of the brass casing, were first made in Birmingham in c.1790 by John Linwood in St Paul's Square.

Stamped brasswork was another specialist area. It had originated with a patent taken out by John Pickering, a London jeweller, in 1769, for a machine which stamped thin sheet metal between dies bearing the shape of the finished article. The principle was soon adapted in Birmingham, where, the same year, Richard Ford patented a

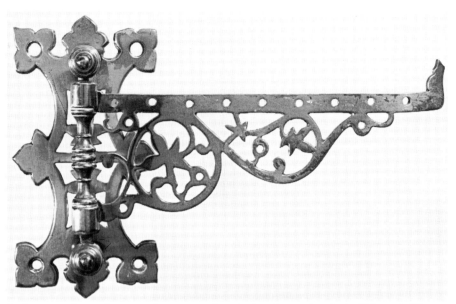

Jack crane of cast brass used to suspend a clockwork roasting jack. Wilcox & Pitman, brassfounders of Henrietta Street, Birmingham, registered this ivy-leaf design in 1889.

new method of raising saucepans, warming pans, basins, scales and kettles by stamping. Fine-gauge rolled sheet brass was used to stamp out coffin furniture, and articles such as cornice pole ends, buttons and buckles, previously made by casting, could now be made more quickly and cheaply by stamping.

Several other new processes using sheet brass were added to the Birmingham industry in the nineteenth century. Iron tube cased in brass was introduced in 1803 and used in huge quantities for picture rods, railings and brass bedsteads, which became popular from the 1840s. In 1838 Charles Green perfected a method of making seamless brass tube: stronger than the tube made by the older method of drawing from flat strips soldered along the seam, it was soon adopted for steam-engine boilers. Later in the century, spinning was introduced to make holloware by raising sheet metal against a revolving chuck.

The technical developments widened the demand for brass: it was cheaper than ever and the Birmingham industry continued to grow. By 1865, 38,000 tons of copper, zinc and old brass were consumed annually by 216 manufacturers. The average workforce had grown to between two and three hundred. Small, low-roofed and badly lit workshops, typical of foundries in 1800, had in most instances been replaced by large well-ventilated factories, with steam-powered lathes replacing those operated by treadle. Birmingham had become the city of brass – its products were found in every part of the world and virtually every walk of life.

Trade card of Emerson & Howell, brassfounders of 81 Temple Street, Bristol, from 1819 to 1831. Like many nineteenth-century general founders, they made cocks, pumps and sanitary ware.

UTILITY AND ORNAMENT

In Victorian Britain the applications of brass were almost endless; with physical qualities of toughness, hardness and colour which varied according to the zinc content, brass was extremely versatile and inexpensive. The uses ranged from utility to ornament – from engineers' grease cups to hearth furniture – although with brassware it was often difficult to separate function from ornament.

Much of the nineteenth-century expansion of the industry was fuelled by the growing demand for brass in plumbing and engineering. The increase in the manufacture of plumbers' accessories was directly related to the Public Health Act of 1848, which rapidly brought about improvements in domestic water supply and sanitation. Soon plumbers' brassfounders were advertising a wide range of fittings for baths, wash-basins and toilet cisterns.

As the use of steam power spread in the nineteenth century, founders established new business making steam cocks, whistles and gauges; they were made of an alloy of copper, brass and tin called gunmetal, capable of withstanding pressure and heat. From the 1840s rolled sheet brass was used to make the chimney caps, dome covers and decorative beadings for the growing numbers of railway locomotives. Seamless brass tube was used in large quantities for the boilers of both locomotives and ships. Other brass manufacturers specialised in the large range of fittings in brass sold by ship's chandlers.

London had long been the centre for the making of scientific instruments. Precision instruments for navigation and surveying and optical equipment such as microscopes and telescopes relied heavily on brass. Clock movements and balance scales, where accuracy was vital, were also made in brass: scales and weights were made for many uses, including letter scales for post offices following the

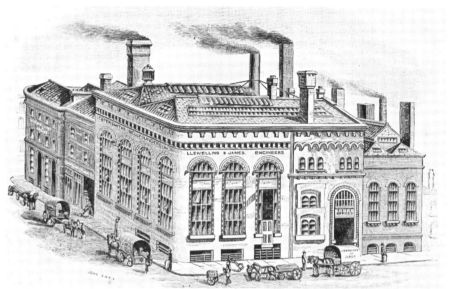

A view of Llewellins & James's foundry at Castle Green, Bristol, from their 1889 catalogue. By then the largest brassfounders in Bristol, they made a wide range of brass and copper ware including domestic utensils, gaslight and plumbing accessories, bells and engineering components.

Right: *'Maslin kettle', cast brass with wrought-iron bail handle.*

Below: *Bib tap, cast brass, early twentieth century.*

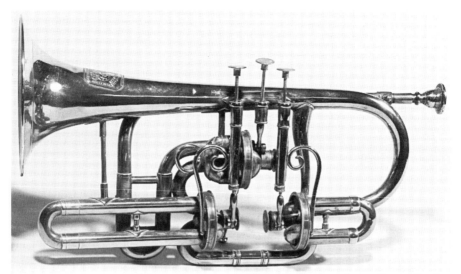

Cornet or 'cornopean' made by John Augustus Köhler of 35 Henrietta Street, Covent Garden, London, c.1840. In 1838 Kohler had acquired the rights to Shaw's patent swivel disc valves, which were applied to this instrument.

introduction of the penny post in 1840.

In the nineteenth century technological improvements to brass musical instruments stimulated the rise of brass bands. The perfection of the valve from the 1830s increased the versatility of existing instruments such as the French horn and trumpet and led to the introduction of new instruments, the 'cornopean', or cornet, for example, whilst others like the bass horn and the ophicleide were made obsolete by the tuba and the euphonium.

For kitchen use, the manufacture of brass bottle jacks remained an important specialist manufacture throughout the nineteenth century, especially in Birmingham, where in the 1860s forty thousand jacks were produced annually. The use of brass in the kitchen, however, declined in the nineteenth century in the face of competition from cast iron, tinplate and copper. By the end of the nineteenth century brass pans were considered old-fashioned and only brass preserving pans – 'maslin kettles' – remained in general use.

Many hearth accessories were made in brass: fenders, trivets, fire irons and coal scuttles. The introduction of the wide crinoline dress after 1850 increased the demand for brass fire guards from Birmingham. Later in the century another fashion, that for tiled hearths and kerbs, caused the decline of brass fenders. Then, in the early 1900s, firegrates were frequently embellished with sheet-brass or copper canopies pressed with *art nouveau* designs.

The association of brass with lighting appliances continued. In Birmingham heavily knopped candlesticks on square and octagonal bases were made for most of the nineteenth century. Inevitably, this branch of the trade suffered a relative decline as oil and gas lighting increased but in the second half of the nineteenth century candlestick makers found new business making sconces for 'cottage' pianos. In London attractive brass candle lamps with etched glass shades made at the Clerkenwell works of William Palmer enjoyed two decades of popularity following their introduction in 1832. In time they, too, succumbed to cheaper and brighter oil lamps.

Simple spout oil lamps with a solid wick were made in sheet brass in the eight-

Trade advertisement of W. Blakeway & Son, manufacturer of brass and japanned iron lamps and lanterns, Edgbaston Street, Birmingham. From Wrightson's 'Triennial Directory of Birmingham', 1818.

eenth century. In 1785 Matthew Boulton started manufacturing 'Argand' lamps at his Soho factory in Birmingham. Named after its Swiss inventor, the Argand lamp was far superior to the old lamps, having a hollow wick and a glass chimney which improved the air supply so the flame burned brighter. Other improved oil lamps followed, such as the 'Moderator'. But they were expensive and difficult to maintain and it was not until the introduction of the paraffin lamp after 1859 that oil lighting became simple and affordable enough to attract a mass market. In 1859 Syson Nibbs started making cheap flat-wicked paraffin lamps in Birmingham and in 1865 Joseph Hinks began production

of his highly successful 'Duplex' lamp with a double burner at the Crystal Lamp Works. In that year W. C. Aitken calculated that 75,000 brass paraffin lamps and some 500,000 stamped brass burners were manufactured in Birmingham.

Gas had first been demonstrated as a practical form of lighting by William Murdoch, an employee of Matthew Boulton, in 1792. In 1803 the Soho factory was lit by gas and in 1810 Messenger of Broad Street started the production of brass gas fittings in Birmingham. Before long, the manufacture of gas burners, taps and lamps ranging from simple bracket lamps to gaseliers – gas-lit chandeliers – became a separate branch of the trade. By

'Matador' paraffin lamp with central draught burner and mirror reflector.

1833 there were five manufacturers of gas fittings listed in local trade directories; by 1865 the number had risen to twenty-five.

Cabinet brassfoundry was an important part of the Birmingham industry in the nineteenth century. An enormous range of fittings in cast and pressed brass was available: castors, hinges, screws, bolts, latches and furniture handles of many styles. There were also varieties of hat and coat hooks and brassware for carpets, curtains and picture hanging. Locks ranged from small mortice locks for trunks and cabinets to heavy rim locks for house doors. Brass competed with cast iron for other items of door furniture: knobs and knockers, kick plates, key escutcheons and, from 1840, letter-box plates.

Candle lamp, cast brass with etched glass shade, bearing the brass label of William Palmer, Clerkenwell, London, c.1832-60.

Door knocker, cast brass, c.1850-75.

Public-house tobacco box; inserting a penny in the slot opened the lid to the tobacco. This one was made by Rich, a Bridgwater brassfounder, c.1840; it is inscribed with the name W. Burnett, landlord of the Bunch of Grapes, Milk Street, Bristol, between 1842 and 1843.

From the early eighteenth century plaques, badges and tipstaves had been made in brass as marks of authority. In the early nineteenth century, members of village friendly societies in the West Country carried ceremonial staves capped with ornamental brasses made in Bristol and probably also in Bridgwater, Somerset. Each society was identified by its own distinctive emblem and several hundred are known. Victorian police constables were often issued with short brass

Badge of a port of Bristol porter (docker) bearing the arms of the city of Bristol on the front and the name of the porter, W. Smith, and the date, 1790, on the reverse.

Parish constable's tipstaff from St James Ward, Bristol, 1826.

tipstaves as tokens of office.

Brass served decorative functions in many other areas of public life. In the middle decades of the nineteenth century there was a revival of church memorials made of brass, inspired by renewed interest in medieval art. A revolution in retailing after 1850 brought not only more shops but higher standards of window display: brass nameplates, sash bars and furnishings such as display stands for merchandise and counter railings of brass tube became fashionable whilst the interiors of late Victorian public houses sparkled with polished beer engines, gas lamps and other fittings of brass.

In Victorian times, too, brass rose in popularity as an embellishment to horse harness. In the eighteenth century it had been customary to suspend a single brass on the forehead of a carthorse and after c.1830 the decoration spread to ear brasses, the martingale, to which as many as ten brasses were attached, and brasses each side of the runners at the shoulders. Fly terrets of brass completed the effect. Earlier horse brasses were cast whilst after c.1870 many were stamped from sheet metal. Hundreds of designs are known based on the sun, moon, hearts, animals and birds; windmills, steam locomotives and royal events were also popular subjects.

Purely ornamental pieces were made by nineteenth-century founders, braziers and fettlers using odd scraps of brass in the workshop. Animals, miniature pieces of furniture and ladies' boots were cut out of sheet brass to decorate the fireside.

A new dimension to brass as ornament emerged towards the end of the nineteenth century as interest in old brassware caught the attention of collectors. From the 1880s

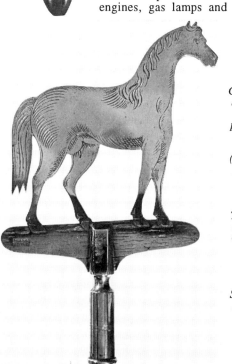

Friendly society brasses, originally fixed to staves carried in procession, were widely found in the West Country. Many of the designs represented the names of the public houses where the societies had their headquarters. (Left) Emblem of the Hambrook Society, Gloucestershire, which met at the White Horse Inn. This brass of c.1850 is stamped 'Hale & Co.', brassfounders of Narrow Wine Street, Bristol. (Right) Emblem of the Fishponds Society, Gloucestershire, which met at the Full Moon.

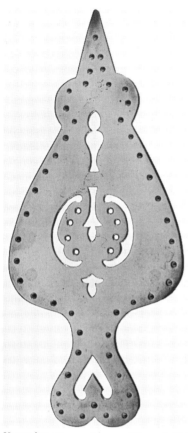

The combination of utility and ornament is shown well here in this laundry iron stand of cast brass, nineteenth century.

a craze for collecting horse brasses stimulated the making of commemorative issues marking royal jubilees and other events. The manufacturers were not slow to see a new opportunity and from the 1890s replicas of old brass utensils were manufactured, notably by Pearson Page of Birmingham.

After 1900 the functional role of brass was eroded by competition from new materials such as stainless steel and bakelite which were easier to keep clean. At work and at home, the time-consuming cleaning of brass was increasingly viewed as a disadvantage as labour costs rose. Bathroom and kitchen fittings, whilst still made of brass, were more likely to be nickel- or chrome-plated although elsewhere in the home brass still filled a decorative role. In the 1920s and 1930s suburbia adopted brass to help create the cosy cottage atmosphere fashionable in the mock-Tudor semi-detached house. Reproduction warming pans and skimmers were displayed in the oak-panelled hallways whilst new articles of brass were introduced for the living room: cigarette boxes, jardinieres, magazine racks and gongs, crumb and tea trays, which were often given a hammered finish. There was, be-

Horse brasses, cast brass. (From left) Inscribed 'J. Bool Builder & Co. Bath 1872'; star and crescent moons design; inscribed 'E. Olding Ratfin Farm 1857'.

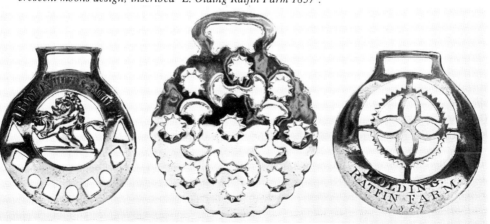

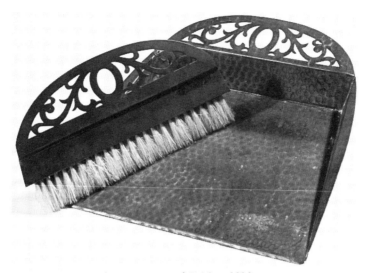

Crumb brush and tray, sheet brass, hammered finish, c.1920s.

sides, a seemingly endless range of small brass knick-knacks: bells, ash trays and mantelpiece ornaments of every kind, many imported from the Far East. These ensured the popularity of brass remained undiminished throughout the twentieth century.

Indian 'elephant' bell, cast brass with inlaid red paint; a fireside ornament in the West Yorkshire home of the author's grandmother, Elizabeth Eveleigh, c.1950-71.

GLOSSARY OF BRASSES AND RELATED COPPER ALLOYS

Bell-metal: alloy of 80 per cent copper and 20 per cent tin.

Brass: alloy of copper and zinc with generally between 60 and 80 per cent copper and between 40 and 20 per cent zinc.

Bronze: alloy of copper and varying proportions of tin; some bronzes contain other metals such as phosphorus, depending on application.

Calamine: zinc carbonate ($ZnCO_3$), an ore of zinc found in carboniferous limestone regions.

Calamine brass: brass made by smelting calcined calamine with broken or granulated copper; maximum zinc content 28 per cent.

Crock brass: old name for copper-lead alloy used mainly for casting domestic utensils.

Gun-metal: alloy of copper (80 per cent), yellow brass (9 per cent), tin (10 per cent) and lead (1 per cent). The mixture can vary.

Latten: old name for brass usually in sheet form and including the metal of medieval church brasses, which sometimes had small quantities of tin added for hardness.

Kettle brass: old name for sheet brass used for battery ware.

Muntz's metal: alloy of copper (60 per cent) and zinc (40 per cent) patented by G. F. Muntz in 1832 for sheathing the wooden hulls of ships.

Paktong: alloy of copper, zinc and nickel, of Chinese origin, resembling silver; used in eighteenth-century England as a cheaper alternative to silver.

Pinchbeck: golden coloured low-zinc brass invented by Christopher Pinchbeck (*c.*1670-1732.)

Pot-metal: alloy of copper and lead.

Shruff: waste brass.

Spelter: old name for zinc.

Tombac: golden-coloured low zinc brass.

Tutenag: alternative name for spelter (zinc).

Yellow brass: old name for general foundry brass often containing up to 3 per cent lead to aid casting and machining.

FURTHER READING

Aitken, W. C. 'Brass and Brass Manufactures' in S. Timmins, *Birmingham and the Midland Hardware District*. Hardwick, 1866.

Brears, P. *North Country Folk Art*. John Donald, 1989.

Burgess, F. W. *Chats on Old Copper and Brass*. T. Fisher Unwin, 1914.

Burke, J. *Birmingham Brass Candlesticks*. University of Virginia, 1986.

Day, J. *Bristol Brass. The History of the Industry*. David & Charles, 1973.

Day, J. 'Copper, Zinc and Brass' in J. Day and R. F. Tylecote, *The Industrial Revolution in Metals*. Institute of Metals, 1991.

Eveleigh, D. J. *Cooking Pots and Old Curios – the Posnet and Skillet*. Folk Life, 1994.

Field, R., and Gentle, R. *English Domestic Brass*. Elek, 1975.

Gates, P. *The Brass Founders' and Finishers' Manual*. Crosby Lockwood & Son, 1926.

Haedeke, H. *Metalwork*. Weidenfeld & Nicolson, 1970.

Hamilton, H. *The English Copper and Brass Industries to 1800*. Longman, 1926.

Horner, J. G. *Brassfounding*. Elmot, 1918.

Hornsby, P. *Collecting Antique Copper and Brass*. Morland, 1989.

Michaelis, R. F. *Old Domestic Base Metal Candlesticks*. Antique Collectors Club, 1978.

Schiffer, P., N. and H. *The Brass Book*. Schiffer, 1978.

Seymour Lindsay, J. *Iron and Brass Implements of the English House*. Medici, 1927.

Snodin, M. *Old Base Metal Spoons*. Batsford, 1908.

Victoria and Albert Museum. *Old English Pattern Books of the Metal Trades* (catalogue). HMSO, 1913.

Vince, J. *Discovering Horse Brasses*. Shire, 1968; reprinted 1994.

Wills, G. *Collecting Copper and Brass*. Avco, 1962.

PLACES TO VISIT

Intending visitors are advised to check before making a special journey whether relevant items are on display and to find out the opening times.

Bath Industrial Heritage Centre, Camden Works, Julian Road, Bath, Avon BA1 2RH. Telephone: 01225 318348.

Blaise Castle House Museum, Henbury, Bristol, Avon BS10 7QS. Telephone: 0117 950 6789.

Bewdley Museum, The Shambles, Load Street, Bewdley, Worcestershire DY12 2AE. Telephone: 01299 403573.

The Black Country Museum, Tipton Road, Dudley, West Midlands DY1 4SQ. Telephone: 0121-557 9643.

Royal Albert Memorial Museum, Queen Street, Exeter, Devon EX4 3RX. Telephone: 01392 265858.

York Castle Museum, Tower Street, York, North Yorkshire YO1 1RY. Telephone: 01904 653611.